KU-575-582

TALKING IT THROUGH

Be Careful

Althea

Illustrated by Ian Newsham

Happy Cat Books

Helen and Eliat are playing houses at play-school. Helen stops her teddy from climbing up to reach the top shelf. Helen knows it is dangerous. She hurt her head when she fell off the chair at home.

Careful Ted! You might fall and hurt yourself.

Eliat is doing the ironing. There is a knock at the door. Eliat can't leave his teddy on his own. He might pull the iron down and burn himself.

Helen, look after teddy for me, while I answer the door.

Both Helen and Eliat have younger sisters, so they know about being careful when cooking.
Sally has come to play too. She lays the table. She gives the teddies spoons. Eliat and Helen cook the dinner.

You can't have a knife yet. You are not old enough. You might cut yourself.

Later, Sally and Helen bath their dolls.

Stay with the dolls while I fetch the shampoo. They mustn't slip under the water and drown.

They wash the dolls' hair.

Don't be silly.

Helen says that she is not being silly. "Mum said that if anyone tried to touch me in my private places, I could shout 'stop that's rude.' She said that I was to tell her about it."

After play-school Eliat and Sally are going to play at Helen's house. Helen's mum comes to fetch them. They hold hands to cross the road to the park.

Can we pat your dog, please, Mr Bell?

Helen's mum tells Eliat not to pat the dog.

You must always ask the owner if the dog is friendly. Some dogs don't like to be petted.

Woof, woof

Mr Bell says, "Yes he likes children, but one at a time. Make a fist and let him sniff your hand first, so he can get to know you."

Helen's mum has brought some bread, so they can feed the ducks.

Helen's mum explains that water can be dangerous. Never play too close to it, unless you are with an adult.

You might drown if you fell in. It's lucky I'm here to look after you.

At home, Amy wants to join in all the games. The others say she is too young for snakes and ladders.

Amy gets out her trike. She knows she's not allowed to ride so fast indoors. She might crash and hurt herself, or somebody else.

Be careful, Amy! You know what mum will say.

Sally's dad has told her never to eat anything in the garden, without asking first. Some berries can make you very ill.

Later they have a tea party for all their dolls and teddies. First they make them wash their hands.

Mum has lit the fire, and put the guard in front of it. Sally doesn't like her teddy to go too near the fire. He might singe his fur.

Be careful of your mug. Ted might tip it over and scald himself.

Helen has heard her mum saying that hot drinks can scald you.

Helen's mum comes in and tells them to put their toys away, and to get ready for their tea.

Helen's mum straps Amy into her chair.

Yes, but be very careful. The knife is sharp.

At tea Eliat tells them about when his sister almost ate some pills. "She found them at Aunty's and she thought they were sweets! Mum and dad keep pills and medicines in a cupboard high up on the wall, so my sister and I can't reach them. They might make you very ill."

Helen's mum says they keep all their garden tools and sprays locked in the shed, so Amy won't find them by mistake.

After tea Helen's mum shows them how to make paper dolls. Amy watches. She is not big enough to use the scissors yet.

They decide to have a game of hide and seek
before Eliat and Sally have to go home.

Helen's mum comes in. "Put those matches down at once. You know you are not allowed to play with matches or candles. You might start a fire."

Sally says she is very sorry. She knew it was wrong really. Helen's mum gives her a torch.

You can use this to find Eliat.

After Eliat and Sally have gone home,
Helen helps her mum tidy up. Mum
says it's not a good idea for Helen to
have her toys on the stairs.

There is a gate on the stairs to stop
Amy from climbing up on her own.
Amy is learning to bump down the
stairs on her bottom. She is getting
good at it.

Helen is always having to tell her teddy to take care. It's because she doesn't want him to get hurt.

Notes for parents

This helpful book deals with safety in the home in a practical and common sense way that young children can understand and apply to the things that they (and their younger sisters and brothers) do.

Responsibility for safety in the home rests with the adults in the family, of course, and it is important to remember that children will imitate the way you do things and adopt your attitude to safety.

Particular care should be taken to:

1 Lock away household cleaning fluids, medicines, matches and sharp objects.
2 Keep hot drinks and teapots out of reach and keep children away from hot surfaces (eg. a hot oven door) and unguarded fires. Use fireguards on all types of fires.
3 Use coiled flexes that will not hang down within a child's reach on kettles and coffee machines. Never leave an iron unattended - a child can easily pull the flex.
4 Use safety covers on all unused electrical sockets.
5 Use gates at the top and bottom of stairs if you have a toddler or a crawling baby. Teach your child to climb and descend stairs safely.
6 Fix window locks to prevent children from opening them too widely and falling out.
7 Always supervise water play.

We all want our homes to be safe and secure for children and with a little care they will be.

This Happy Cat book has been produced in co-operation with The Royal Society for the Prevention of Accidents. If you would like more information about helping your child with safety education write to: Safety Education Department, **RoSPA**, RoSPA House, Edgbaston Park, 353 Bristol Road, Birmingham B5 7ST.